David and Angus Drummon
David is ten and Angus is ei
The school is closing now.
They are going home.

David and Angus live in an old house.
Their father is a fisherman.
He has a small boat.
It is in the harbour.

'Hello Dad!' Angus shouts. 'We're home!'

live    sea   boat   harbour   fisherman

The two boys get up and go to the window.
They look out and smile. The sun is out.

'Can we come out in the boat?' says David.

Grandfather looks at the boys. He smiles.
'Yes,' says their father. 'You can come and help us.'

2

Grandfather   smile   get up

The boat is in the harbour.
Its name is the 'Water-wheel'.

'Come on boys!' says Mr Drummond. 'Jump in!'
'Have a good time!' Mrs Drummond shouts.

The sun is out. The sea is blue.
The 'Water-wheel' moves out of the harbour.
David and Angus are happy.

jump in

The boat goes out into the open sea.
'It's time for the net!' says Mr Drummond.

He stops the boat. 'Come on boys. Help me.'

The big net is in the water.
Mr Drummond holds the wheel and drives the boat.

net   water   wheel

It is time for the net to come in. There are fish in it.

'Look Dad!' David shouts. 'What's that?'

'A dolphin!' shouts Angus.
'There's a dolphin in our net!'

'Stop!' says Grandfather. He points to the dolphin.
'Look! The net's cutting him!'

fish　　　dolphin　cutting

5

Mr Drummond jumps into the sea.
He takes his knife and cuts the net.
Grandfather helps.

David and Angus watch.

The dolphin jumps out.
'Good! Good!' shout David and Angus.

The dolphin swims out into the sea.
It has a smile on its face.

6

jumps out   knife

The boys watch the dolphin.
But Dad and Grandfather look at the net.
It has holes in it and no fish.

David and Angus come to look at the net.

'No fish!' they say.
'Not one,' says Grandfather.

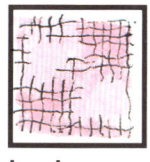

holes

The Drummonds go back to the harbour.
It is cold and Mr Drummond is wet.

'Come on Dad,' says David.
'Time to go home.'

Mr Drummond stands near the fire.

'You look ill,' says Mrs Drummond.
'Yes,' he says, 'I am.'

wet    ill    fire

Mr Drummond is ill. He goes to bed.
David makes him a cup of tea.
Angus gives him an orange and a
box of paper handkerchiefs.

It is half past seven and the Drummonds are eating.

Angus points to his plate. 'No fish!' he says.
'No, our fish are in the sea!' says David.

bed

9

Mrs Drummond and Grandfather work on the net.
'We can buy a net,' says Grandfather.
'No we can't,' says Mrs Drummond.
'Nets are expensive'.

The fishermen are going out to sea.
But the 'Water-wheel' can't go out.

'Come on!' David says to Angus.
They go behind the house.
'Look! We can help. We can go fishing.'

'We're going fishing, Mum,' says David.
'Going fishing?' says Grandfather. 'Oh good!'

'Yes. Fish for dinner!' says Angus.
'Oh good!' Grandfather smiles.

dinner   go fishing

David and Angus go to the harbour.
They sit on the wall.
'Come on fish ... ' says Angus.

Old Jimmy watches them.
'There are no fish down there,' he says.

'No fish!' says Angus. He is sad.

Old Jimmy points to his boat. 'Look! There's my boat. You can take it and fish in the harbour.'

12

sit

wall

'Thanks, Jimmy,' say the boys. They go down to the small boat.

Old Jimmy watches them. He sees them go out into the harbour.

'Yes! There are fish here!' shouts Angus. 'Look Jimmy!' He holds up a big fish.

Jimmy smiles. He sees them. He sees the fish.

13

Angus looks at the sky.
'It's cold,' he says. 'Can we go home now?'

'What a big fish!' shouts David.
He stands up. 'Help me Angus!'

'Here it is!' shouts David.
Angus is standing behind
him. 'Ah!' he cries.

Now the boat goes out
of the harbour and into
the sea.

'I can't move the boat,' says David.
'Help!' shouts Angus. 'Help!'
But there are no boats near.

'Look!' shouts Angus. 'A dolphin!'
The dolphin swims near the boat.

'Look! It has a cut! It's the dolphin! It's our dolphin!'

The dolphin pushes the boat.

'What is he doing?' says David.

The life-ring goes into the water.

The dolphin drops the life-ring back into the boat.

The dolphin pushes his nose into the life-ring.

'The rope!' shouts Angus.

16

life-ring rope

The dolphin helps the two boys.
He takes them to the harbour.

'This is good!' Angus laughs.
'Look!' says David. 'I can see Grandfather and Mum.'

The boat is at the steps now.
'Oh David! Angus! You're back!'
cries their mother.

She is very happy to see them.
'Look at our fish!' says Angus.

steps

It is time to go home.
'Fish for dinner!' smiles Grandfather.
'Big fish,' laughs Mrs Drummond.

David and Angus look at the sea.
'Where's the dolphin?' says David.

'There!' Angus points.
They see him now. He is jumping out of the water.
He is saying goodbye.

saying goodbye

Words in this book

bed	boat	cutting	dinner

dolphin	fire	fish	fisherman

get up	go fishing	Grandfather	harbour
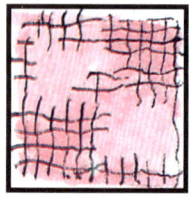			
holes	ill	jump in	jumps out

Questions

Where are the boys and Grandfather?
Where is the boat?
How many people?
How many dolphins?

What is his name?   What colour is the sea?
How old is he?
Is he smiling?   Is Grandfather
What is he doing?   a fisherman?

What is his name?
How old is he?   What are these?

What is in the net?
Is it big or small?

How many people?
How many boats?

Is the boat in the harbour?
What colour is it?
Is it small?

What is this?

Are David and Angus hungry?
Are they happy?

What is this?
Is it big?
Is it for dinner?

Who is this?
Is she sad?
Is she saying goodbye?

Is the dolphin
coming or going?
Is he happy?
Where is he?

Oxford University Press
Walton Street, Oxford OX2 6DP

Oxford New York Toronto Madrid Mebourne Auckland
Kuala Lumpur Singapore Hong Kong Tokyo Delhi
Bombay Calcutta Madras Niarobi
Dar es Salaam Cape Town

and associated companies in
Berlin Ibadan

OXFORD and OXFORD ENGLISH
are trade marks of Oxford University Press

ISBN 0 19 422425 2

© Oxford University Press 1993

All rights reserved. No part of this publication may be
reproduced, stored in a retrieval system, or transmitted, in any
form or by any means, electronic, mechanical, photocopying,
recording, or otherwise, without the prior permission of
Oxford Universty Press.

This book is sold subject to the conditions that it shall not, by
way of trade or otherwise, be lent, re-sold, hired out or otherwise
circulated without the publisher's prior consent in any form of
binding or cover other than that in which it is published and
without a similar condition including this condition being
imposed on the subsequent purchaser.

Illustrated by Alan Marks

Typeset by Creative Intelligence, Bristol, Avon
Printed in Egypt by International Printing House